More True Horse Stories

A Dolch Classic Basic Reading Book

by Edward W. Dolch and Marguerite P. Dolch

illustrated by Meryl Henderson

The Basic Reading Books

The Basic Reading Books are fun reading books that fill the need for easy-to-read stories for the primary grades. The interest appeal of these true stories will encourage independent reading at the early reading levels.

The stories focus on the 95 Common Nouns and the Dolch 220 Basic Sight Vocabulary. Beyond these simple lists, the books use about two or three new words per page.

This series was prepared under the direction and supervision of Edward W. Dolch, Ph.D.

This revision was prepared under the direction and supervision of Eleanor Dolch LaRoy and the Dolch Family Trust.

SRA/McGraw-Hill

*A Division of The **McGraw·Hill** Companies*

Printed in the United States of America.

Send all inquiries to:
SRA/McGraw-Hill
250 Old Wilson Bridge Road, Suite 310
Worthington, OH 43085

ISBN 0-02-830804-2

2 3 4 5 6 7 8 9 0 QST 04 03 02 01 00 99

Table of Contents

The White Horse Patrol

There were many beautiful, white horses in the White Horse Patrol. King was the white horse that led them in the parades.

King loved the parades. He loved the music. He held his head high, and he lifted his feet high as he kept time to the music. He loved to lead the White Horse Patrol.

The White Horse Patrol is made up of men called Shriners. Each man owns a beautiful white horse. Each man has his own work, but part of the time these men ride and train their white horses. They teach the horses to walk by twos, by fours, and by eights. They even teach some of the horses circus tricks.

The White Horse Patrol is sometimes part of the Shriners Circus. The Shriners Circus plays in many cities. It makes money to help children who are sick.

Two of the horses, Silver Lady and Patsy, learned to seesaw. How the children laughed to see two big, white horses on a seesaw. Silver Lady went up and Patsy went down. Then Patsy went up and Silver Lady went down. Silver Lady went up when she lifted her right front leg. Then Patsy lifted her right front leg and went up. The seesaw went up and down.

King, the beautiful horse who led the parades, had the best act in the Shriners Circus.

One day King was in front of the parade going down the street. He was very happy. Children along the street called out to him. The music played. King felt so happy that he stood on his back legs. He began to walk along with his front legs up high.

The children called out, "Look, look. The white horse is walking on his back legs. He is keeping time to the music with his front legs."

From then on, King walked around the circus ring on his back legs. His front legs were up high. It looked as if the horse was keeping time to the music.

No one had to teach King to do this trick. King did this trick all by himself, and when he saw how happy it made the children, he just went on doing it.

Old Dobbin

Dobbin was an old farm horse. He lived on a farm. He always worked hard.

Dobbin was well cared for. He had all he wanted to eat. He had a nice place in the barn to sleep.

All the children on the farm loved old Dobbin. They would sometimes bring the old horse an apple because he loved to eat apples.

Father sometimes let the children ride Old Dobbin. Old Dobbin walked very carefully so that the children would not fall off. Father even let Peter, who was two years old, sit on Old Dobbin. But Father held baby Peter so he would not fall off.

One day Father had come back to the farm driving Old Dobbin. He went into the wagon house and parked the wagon. He took Old Dobbin from the wagon so he could go to his place in the barn. Dobbin went out of the wagon house and started for the barn.

Then Father saw something that frightened him. There, right in the barn door, was baby Peter. Father did not know the baby was around. Old Dobbin would walk right over baby Peter as he went into the building. And Old Dobbin had iron horseshoes on his feet that might hit baby Peter and hurt him.

Father started to call out to Old Dobbin to stop him, but there was no time. Old Dobbin had just got to the barn door and to baby Peter. But Old Dobbin knew that baby Peter was there. He stepped carefully over baby Peter, lifting his feet very high. He did not want to hit baby Peter with his feet.

Father ran and got the baby. Then he and baby Peter went into the barn to talk to Dobbin. Father was glad that Old Dobbin was such a smart old horse. He was glad that Old Dobbin loved the children. Father gave Old Dobbin some oats to eat, and he gave Dobbin an apple, also.

Dan

Dan was a farm horse, and he liked to eat oats. Every night Jim gave Dan a good supper. Jim liked Dan because he was a good horse and he worked hard on the farm.

Every night after he gave Dan his supper, Jim closed the barn door and put a bar across the inside of the door. Then he went out the little barn door.

One morning when Jim went out to the barn, the big barn door was open. Jim thought that Dan might be gone, but Dan was there in his place. Whoever had opened the barn door had not hurt Dan.

That night Jim was very careful to see that the barn door was closed with the bar across the door on the inside. But in the morning, the door was open and the bar was on the ground. Dan was in his place.

Jim could not understand this. Day after day, the door was closed with the bar at night, and it the morning the door would be open with the bar on the ground.

One day the man who lived on the next farm went to Jim's father. The man asked, "Do you know that your horse, Dan, comes over to my farm during the night and eats my oats?"

Jim and his father could not understand how Dan could be in the barn each morning but in the farmer's oats each night. Who was opening the barn door?

"I am going to take my flashlight and sleep in the barn," said Jim to his father. "I am going to find out who is opening the barn door."

Jim went to sleep in the barn. During the night, there was a noise. Jim turned his flashlight on the barn door. There was Dan lifting the bar from the barn door with his teeth.

So that was how it happened. During the night, Dan opened the door, went to the other farm, and ate the oats.

When Jim told his father who was opening the barn door, they both laughed.

"Dan is a smart horse," said Jim's father, "but he must not eat the farmer's oats."

"I will fix that barn door so that Dan cannot open it," said Jim.

Jim and his father put a big bar on the outside of the barn door. That night, Jim closed the barn door and put the big bar across the door on the outside. Dan could not lift it because he could not get to it.

For three nights, the barn door stayed closed, but the next morning Jim found the barn door open. The bar on the outside had been broken.

"I am going to take my flashlight and sleep in the barn again," said Jim. "I am going to find out how that barn door was opened."

Again Jim went to sleep in the barn. During the night, he heard a noise. Jim turned his flashlight on the barn door.

There was Dan with his back to the door. He was pushing and pushing on the door. The bar on the outside of the door broke, and the door opened.

Jim called to Dan and put him back in the barn. Dan did not get to the oats that night.

Jim's father knew that he had to fix that door so Dan could not get out. He got a long iron bar. He put the iron bar across the door on the outside.

That night Jim gave Dan a good supper. Then when he went out, he closed the barn door and put the iron bar across it.

Dan tried pushing the door open, but the iron bar was too strong. The barn door would not open. And Dan did not get to eat the farmer's oats.

Carbine

Carbine was a fine racehorse, and Carbine knew what he wanted. He wanted to win races.

Carbine was a good horse, but when Carbine did not win a race, he became very angry. He would jump around. He would kick and bite.

Sometimes people get angry when they do not win, but they know that they cannot win all the time. They just try harder the next time. But Carbine thought that he could win every race. The people who took care of Carbine would tell him, "Carbine, you just try harder the next time. Then you will win the race."

The people who took care of the horses all loved Carbine. They laughed at his funny ways.

There was one thing that Carbine did not like. He did not like to get his ears wet.

Carbine did not care if his back got wet. He did not care if his legs got wet. But he would not go out in the rain and get his ears wet.

One day there was to be a great race. It started to rain just as it was time for the race. All the other horses were ready for the race, but Carbine would not go out into the rain.

The man who took care of Carbine did not know what to do. He was sure that Carbine could win the race, but Carbine did not like to get his ears wet. He would not go out into the rain.

The man got an umbrella. He walked beside the horse holding the umbrella over the horse's head. This was the only way to get Carbine to go out into the rain.

Everyone laughed when they saw Carbine with the man holding the umbrella over the horse's head.

When Carbine got to the start of the race and saw the other horses, he forgot all about the rain. Carbine wanted to win. He forgot all about his ears. Carbine ran and won the race.

The man who took care of him made a little umbrella. He fixed the umbrella on Carbine's head. It just covered his ears. It was very funny to see this beautiful racehorse on a rainy day. Oh, how fast he could run with his little umbrella keeping his ears from getting wet.

Black Gold

U-See-It was a horse owned by Al Hoots, who lived on a farm in Oklahoma. U-See-It had a little, black colt named Black Gold. Al named the colt for the oil that had been found on his farm, and oil is called black gold.

U-See-It had won some races, and Al Hoots was sure that her colt, Black Gold, was going to grow up to be a fine racehorse.

Black Gold was trained by a man named Webb who had trained U-See-It. Webb talked to the colt, and Black Gold seemed to understand what Webb said to him.

Al Hoots got very sick. He knew that he was going to die. He said to his wife, Rosa, "Never, never sell Black Gold. He is going to grow up to be a fine racehorse. Someday he will win the big race." The big race was the Kentucky Derby.

The oil on Al Hoots's farm made Rosa much money. She had money to take Black Gold and his trainer, Webb, to any race in the country.

Black Gold began to win. Everyone talked about the black horse that Rosa owned. He was a fine racehorse.

And then came the big race, the Kentucky Derby.

Before Al Hoots died, Rosa told him that she would take care of Black Gold. Someday she would take him to the big race. That day had come.

Webb, in an old raincoat that he always wore, was with Black Gold. "Now, my baby," said Webb into Black Gold's ear, "this is the big day. Your mother was a good racehorse, but you are better than your mother was. Al Hoots said before he died that you would win the big race. Now this is the day. You just have to win."

Black Gold looked at Webb as if he knew what Webb was saying to him.

Rosa Hoots was in a box seat at the Kentucky Derby. She was thinking of what Al had said to her before he died, "Someday Black Gold will win the big race."

The horses were ready for the race. Some of the horses were jumping around, but Black Gold was very good. He liked the man who was riding him. He did just what he was told to do.

At last the horses were off. Black Gold was not ahead. Two horses were ahead of him, and he could not get by them.

The horses were running very fast. It was a long race. Two horses were still ahead of Black Gold.

The horses were at the last of the race. The man riding on Black Gold talked to him. Black Gold knew what the man wanted him to do.

Black Gold ran around one horse. All the horses were running as fast as they could. Only one horse was ahead of Black Gold. Black Gold ran ahead of that horse. Black Gold won the Kentucky Derby.

Webb watched the race without a smile. Rosa Hoots watched the race without a smile. They were thinking about Al Hoots. How happy Al had been when U-See-It had won races. How happy Al would have been to know that U-See-It's black colt had won the Kentucky Derby.

Black Gold held his head high when they put the red roses on him, as they always do for the winner of the Kentucky Derby. The trainer, Webb, in his old raincoat, and Rosa stood beside the black horse. They knew that Al would have been so happy to be there.

Prince Hal

Prince Hal was a beautiful horse. He had been trained to jump over high fences. He was the best jumper in England, France, and the United States.

Prince Hal knew just what he wanted to do. But his owner, Pat Smythe, knew that a jumper must always do just what his rider tells him to do. So she had to train Prince Hal carefully, and she had to train him for a long time. Even after Prince Hal won many horse shows, he still had to go to jumping school.

Every morning after breakfast, Prince Hal was brushed and made ready to go to jumping school because Prince Hal had to learn many things before he became the best jumper in England.

Most horses like to run in the morning. They like to turn and jump as their riders tell them to. But not Prince Hal. In the morning, Prince Hal did not want to do any of the things other horses want to do.

After breakfast, Prince Hal was sleepy. After he was brushed to go out, the beautiful horse lay down and went to sleep again. Then the people who took care of the horses had to brush him all over again.

When, at last, Prince Hal went out for his morning practice, he could hardly walk. The other horses were out running and having a good time. But Prince Hal just stood with his head hanging down and his eyes almost closed. He looked very tired. You would never think that this horse would ever be the best jumper in England.

But when Prince Hal was at a horse show, he was not the same horse. He held his head up. He looked at everything around him. He looked carefully at the fences he was going to jump over. He seemed to be thinking how high they were. How beautiful Prince Hal looked as he jumped over the fences! He jumped over higher fences than the other horses did, and he looked very beautiful.

The morning after a horse show, Prince Hal always looked tired and sleepy. He did not look like a jumper at all.

Prince Hal liked to tease. Sometimes he teased his owner, Pat. After jumping all the fences at a horse show and being the best horse in the show, he tried to throw Pat off his back. Pat was such a good rider that Prince Hal never threw her. Prince Hal seemed to be saying, "Look here, Pat. I jumped over all those fences just like you wanted me to. Now I am going to do just what I want to do."

When Prince Hal was at home, he sometimes teased Pat. One day when she was patting him, he bit the buttons off her coat. Then he held the buttons in his mouth and looked as if he had done nothing at all.

One day Prince Hal needed new horseshoes. He stood very quietly beside the blacksmith as the blacksmith worked hard putting on the new horseshoes.

Prince Hal must have thought that the blacksmith had something funny across his back. It was his suspenders. Prince Hal watched the suspenders.

When no one was looking, Prince Hal took the suspenders in his teeth and pulled them out as far as they would go. Then suddenly he let them go.

The blacksmith jumped when the suspenders hit his back. But when he looked up, Prince Hal was looking the other way as if he had done nothing at all.

The Long, Long Walk

You might think that a mile is a long way to walk. If you were to walk a hundred miles, you would think that was a very long walk.

Mancha was a South American horse. He walked 10,000 miles. He walked up and down high mountains. He walked through great woods where there were many kinds of wild animals. But the part of his long, long walk that Mancha did not like at all was his walk down the streets of New York City. He did not like the hard streets. He did not like so many people. He did not like the noise that the cars made.

Mancha, Gato, and Mr. Tschiffely started their trip from Buenos Aires in South America. It took over two years for Mancha, Gato, and Mr. Tschiffely to get from Buenos Aires to New York City. It was a long, long walk of 10,000 miles.

Mr. A. E. Tschiffely was a teacher. Part of each year he went out with the cowhands of South America. The ponies he and the cowhands rode were small and strong. Mr. Tschiffely got to thinking that he would like to ride a South American cow pony from Buenos Aires to New York City.

A good friend who had many cow ponies gave Mr. Tschiffely Mancha and Gato. Mancha was a brown-and-white horse. He was very smart and very wild. He held his head high and looked at everything around him.

Mancha would only let Mr. Tschiffely ride him. When he found that he could not throw Mr. Tschiffely, he became a very good horse.

Gato was a wild horse, too, but he was more quiet than Mancha. Gato was a good packhorse. He followed behind Mancha because Mancha always wanted to go first.

One day Mr. Tschiffely was walking along a little mountain road. Mancha was walking behind him, and then came Gato, the packhorse. Suddenly, Gato went over the side of the mountain. He would have been killed if a tree had not stopped his fall.

Some people came by and helped Mr. Tschiffely get Gato back up the side of the mountain. They tied ropes around Gato. Then they pulled and pulled. At last Gato was on the road again.

Another time, an Indian had to take Mr. Tschiffely and the two horses across a rope bridge. The rope bridge was across a river up in the mountain. There was no

other way to get across the river. The
bridge was four hundred feet long. Even a
person would be afraid to walk across such
a bridge. Mr. Tschiffely did not know how
he was going to get two horses across the
bridge.

The Indian went first, holding a rope
tied to Mancha's head. Mr. Tschiffely held
Mancha's tail and talked to him all the time
they were walking across the bridge. Once
Mancha stopped when the bridge began
shaking. If the horse had tried to turn

around, he would have gone off the bridge. But Mancha heard Mr. Tschiffely talking to him. When the bridge stopped shaking, he went on. Mancha, the Indian, and Mr. Tschiffely got across the bridge at last.

Then the Indian and Mr. Tschiffely had to go back across the bridge and lead Gato across. Gato was a very quiet horse and went very quietly across the shaking bridge.

Another time Mancha and Gato had to swim across a river. It had rained and rained. The river was full of water. Mr. Tschiffely found an Indian whose work was to help animals get across the river. Many times he took cows across the river.

Many people went to watch the horses swim across the river. It was going to be a very hard swim because the river was so full of water. Some people thought that the horses could not get across. Other people said that the Indian would get the horses across because he knew the river.

The Indian looked at the river very carefully. Then he took the horses into the water. Mancha and Gato could swim, but the water took them down the river. It seemed a very long trip to Mr. Tschiffely, but at last he heard a noise from the people on the other side of the river. He knew that his horses were across.

The Indians would not let Mr. Tschiffely swim across the river because he did not know the bad places in the river. He had to go across the river in a big basket hanging on a rope. The people pulled the basket across the river.

Something very funny happened one day. The horses were going through the woods. Many bugs bit the horses. The horses tried to keep the bugs off with their tails. Mr. Tschiffely wanted to help them.

Mr. Tschiffely tied some colored bird feathers to the horses' tails to help them keep off the bugs.

Mancha looked back to see what Mr. Tschiffely was doing. He saw the colored feathers on the end of his tail. He was so frightened that he ran away. Gato saw the feathers on his tail, too. He ran away after Mancha.

Mr. Tschiffely had a hard time getting his horse back. He never tied feathers to their tails again.

At last Mr. Tschiffely and the two horses got to the United States. Mancha and Gato did not like the hard roads. When they could, they walked on the grass beside the roads.

There were too many cars, and the cars went too fast. One car ran into Mancha and hurt him. It was a good thing that the car did not kill the little horse that had walked so far.

Mr. Tschiffely was afraid that if he had two horses on the road, one of them would be hit. So he left Gato in St. Louis. Then Gato went to New York City by train. Mr. Tschiffely did not need a packhorse for all his things. In the United States he could always find a place to eat and a place to sleep.

Mr. Tschiffely rode Mancha all the way to New York City. That was the end of the 10,000-mile walk.

Mr. Tschiffely told people about his long ride. He told them about his two strong, brave horses. When he got back to South America, he wrote a book about his 10,000-mile trip.

The two brave horses did not stay in New York City, and they did not walk back to Buenos Aires. Mr. Tschiffely took the two horses with him on a ship.

When the ship got to Buenos Aires, Mr. Tschiffely took Mancha and Gato back to their home. They were put in a pasture where they could run and eat as much grass as they wanted to. Their work was done.

The Liberty Horses

Every circus has many horses. The horses do many things. Some of them are workhorses. They pull wagons in the parade before the show starts.

Some of the horses are fine riding horses. They are called "high school" horses. These horses have learned to stand or walk or run just as the rider tells them to. They know how to bow and how to dance to music. High school horses are very beautiful animals.

Then there are horses called "liberty horses" because they do acts in a circus ring without riders. Often ten or more liberty horses will do an act together.

The liberty horses are smart and often very wild. If they get angry, they jump and kick. Their act is wonderful to watch. The trainer stands in the center of the ring with a whip and a stick. He tells the liberty horse what to do by the way he moves the stick or the whip.

When they come into the ring, there are always helpers to watch these beautiful horses and to take them out of the ring when they finish their act.

Sometimes there are both black and white horses in a liberty horse act. Two white horses walk together. Then four white horses walk together and four black horses walk together. Then all the horses run around the ring, in and out, until there is one white, one black, one white, and so on.

One time the liberty horses were about to finish their act. There were ten black horses in the ring. The trainer was in the center of the ring. He had on a red suit.

Five of the beautiful, black horses were going around the ring one way. The other five horses were going around the ring the other way. They were running very fast. It was wonderful to watch those liberty horses going around and around their trainer.

Suddenly something happened that frightened one of the horses. He started to jump and kick. Then all of the other horses started to jump and kick. Around and around the ring the horses ran. Closer and closer the horses moved to the center of the ring. And in the center of the ring was their trainer in his red suit.

The trainer called for help. He was sure that he would be killed because the big horses got closer and closer.

The helpers were in the ring trying to catch the horses. But the horses were so close together and they kicked so much that the helpers could not catch them. The horses became more and more wild as they ran around and around the ring.

The people watching the circus knew that something was not right. They shouted and shouted. And this noise made the horses more wild. No one could get to the trainer. Surely he was going to be killed by the wild liberty horses.

But outside the tent was a very big elephant named Sultan. Sultan liked the trainer of the liberty horses. The trainer always gave Sultan something good to eat.

Sultan heard the noise. He walked into the circus tent to see what was going on. He saw the wild horses. He heard the trainer calling for help.

Sultan walked close to the kicking and jumping horses. He was so big that he just pushed the horses to one side. He put his trunk around the trainer and lifted him high into the air. Then holding the man high in the air, Sultan walked out of the circus ring. Not one of the wild horses could get to the trainer to hurt him.

The horses were afraid of the big elephant. They stopped running. The helpers caught the horses and took them out of the ring. All of the people shouted for Sultan who had saved the trainer.

On the Back of a Horse

This is the story of a little girl named Ella who lived in a circus. When she was three years old, her father put her on a big, white horse. That was the first ride of a little girl who was to grow up to be one of the greatest riders in the world.

Every day Ella rode on the back of the big, white horse. At last she could ride standing on the horse's back.

Soon it came time for Ella to go to school just as other children do. But Ella's school was not like other schools. Her teacher taught her many things out of books. He taught her how to do tricks in the air. A woman who taught the girls in the circus to dance taught Ella to dance, too. And at five years old, Ella was such a good dancer that she danced in the circus. And always, every day, her father taught her more about riding a horse.

Ella had a beautiful sister name Beata who was older than Ella. At every show, Ella watched her sister ride on the back of the big, white horse. Everyone loved Beata, and many people came to the circus just to see Beata ride.

Ella tried to do everything just as her older sister did. She tried to ride just like Beata. She tried to dance just like Beata. She even tried to dance on the back of a horse just like Beata. And she wanted someday for people to come to the circus to see her ride. She hoped that they would give her flowers just like they gave Beata.

One day when Ella was a little over ten years old, she was watching the show of the circus. She had laughed at the clowns as she always did. She had watched the man who was her teacher do his tricks with the yellow balls. He looked very fine in his black-and-white suit. Then it was time for Beata to come into the ring.

Ella always thought that Beata with her pretty, white dress, standing on the back of the white horse, was the most beautiful thing in the world. The people always clapped their hands when Beata rode into the ring. Ella clapped her hands, too.

And then the big, white horse stopped suddenly. It happened so fast that Beata could not catch herself, and she fell to the ground. Ella knew that her sister was hurt because Beata could not get up. The men took Beata from the ring because her legs were hurt.

In a circus, no matter what happens, the show must go on. Ella wanted to go to her sister, but her father put Ella upon the back of the big, white horse. Ella became a circus rider when she was ten years old.

Beata got well and rode a horse in the circus again. Ella rode a horse, too, and she put something new in the act.

Ella had always loved birds. She had ten white birds that she had trained to come and sit on her shoulders. Ella put these ten birds into her circus act.

Ella would ride on the back of the big, white horse. Then she danced on the horse. When the act was over, someone let the white birds out of their cage. As Ella bowed to the people, the birds would fly to her and sit on her shoulders. Everyone would clap and clap. It was the prettiest circus act they had ever seen.

A Fall from a Horse

One night, a man who loved horses went to the New Circus in Paris, France. The New Circus was a very fine circus at that time. The greatest circus acts in the world were part of the New Circus.

The circus was not in a tent but in a very big building. There was just one ring in the building with seats all around it for the people. Right next to the ring there was a row of box seats. The people in the box seats could see the circus best of all because they were right next to the ring.

The best act of that night's show was Ella, who had worked so hard to be one of the greatest circus riders in the world.

A man who loved horses sat in one of the box seats so that he could see the horses in the acts. And he wanted to see Ella ride on her white horse.

The music played and Ella came in all by herself. She had on a long, white dress. All the people clapped, but they wondered how she could do her circus act in a long dress.

Then a beautiful, white horse came into the ring. He went around and around the ring by himself. This was something new, but Ella had trained her horse to do this. Before, there had always been someone to keep the horse going the right way.

Then Ella in her long, white dress ran and jumped up onto the back of the white horse. It was a beautiful act and no woman had ever done anything like that before.

The people clapped and clapped. The white horse, with Ella in her long, white dress standing on its back, went around and around the ring.

Then a lady threw some flowers to Ella. The flowers frightened the white horse, and he jumped to one side. Ella, in the long, white dress, went right over the horse's head.

Everyone thought that Ella would be killed. But Ella went through the air and fell right into the box seat where the man sat. The man caught her, and she was not hurt at all.

That was one fall from a horse that made a circus rider happy because Ella and the man fell in love with each other. In a few years, they were married. The man, who was a very fine rider himself, went with the circus. He became the ringmaster of "The Greatest Show on Earth." And he and Ella lived many, many happy years together.

Whoa, January

There are always clowns in a circus. Children love them and laugh at the funny things the clowns do. And clowns love children.

But being a clown is very hard work. Sometimes clowns will have to practice for a long time to do a kind of fall that will not hurt them. Their act might take only a few minutes, but in that time they have to tell a funny story without saying a word. They tell their stories with their hands and feet and body.

There once was a clown who did an act with an old mule. The mule was named January, which is a funny name for an old mule.

The ringmaster was sitting upon a beautiful, white horse. He blew his whistle. Into the ring came January pulling a red wagon. And in the red wagon was riding a funny-looking clown.

The clown pulled the old mule to a stop and cried out, "Whoa, January." This always made people laugh.

Then the clown got out of his little, red wagon and went to look at the beautiful, white horse. Without saying a thing, he began to act out his story. He told the ringmaster and the people at the circus that he wanted to trade his old mule and red wagon for the beautiful, white horse.

The ringmaster laughed at the thought that he would trade his beautiful, white horse for the old mule. But the clown told the ringmaster about his mule. Remember, he did not say a word. He acted out that his mule was a very smart mule. His mule could bow. His mule could count.

At last the ringmaster traded his white horse for the old mule and the red wagon.

The clown acted very happy. He rode around the circus ring standing on the back of the white horse. You see, the clown was a very good rider.

This happened in the days when many people traded horses. And the people thought it was funny that the ringmaster would trade his beautiful, white horse for the old mule and the red wagon. They always laughed and clapped their hands as the clown rode out of the ring standing on the back of the white horse.

Then the fun would start. The ringmaster cracked his long, black whip, but he could not make the old mule move. He could not get him out of the ring so that the next circus act could come on. He cracked his whip and he pulled the mule, but the mule was trained not to move.

Then the ringmaster had to call the funny clown to come back and get his old mule out of the circus ring.

The funny clown came back riding on the white horse. But he would not give the white horse back to the ringmaster. Without saying a thing, he told the ringmaster that they had traded the mule for the white horse, and the white horse was his.

Then the ringmaster told the clown that he could keep the white horse if he would get the old mule and the red wagon out of the ring so the other acts could go on.

But the clown showed that he was afraid to get off the white horse because he thought the ringmaster would take the white horse away from him.

At last the ringmaster took a lot of money out of his pocket. He told the clown that he could keep the white horse and he could keep all of the money if only he would take the old mule and the red wagon out of the circus ring.

The clown got down from the beautiful, white horse and tied him to the back of the little, red wagon. He put the money into his pocket. Then he got into the little, red wagon. Away went the funny clown with the old mule and the little, red wagon and the beautiful, white horse.

And that is the story that the clown told the people at the circus without saying anything.

a	bad	broke
about	balls	broken
across	bar	brush
act	barn	brushed
acted	basket	Buenos Aires
acts	be	bugs
afraid	Beata	building
after	beautiful	but
again	became	buttons
ahead	because	by
air	been	cage
Al	before	call
all	began	called
almost	behind	came
along	being	cannot
always	beside	car
am	best	Carbine
America	better	Carbine's
American	big	care
an	bird	cared
and	birds	careful
angry	bit	carefully
animals	bite	carry
another	black	cars
any	blacksmith	catch
anything	blew	caught
anywhere	body	center
apple	book	children
apples	books	circus
are	both	cities
around	bow	city
as	bowed	clap
asked	box	clapped
at	boxes	close
ate	brave	closed
away	breakfast	closer
baby	bridge	clothes
back	bring	clown

clowns
coat
colored
colt
come
comes
could
count
country
covered
cow
cowhands
cows
cracked
cried
Dan
dance
danced
dancer
day
days
Derby
did
die
died
do
Dobbin
doing
done
door
down
dress
driving
during
each
ear
ears
earth

eat
eats
eights
elephant
Ella
Ella's
end
England
even
ever
every
everyone
everything
eyes
face
fall
far
farm
farmer's
fast
father
feathers
feet
fell
fences
few
find
fine
finish
first
five
fix
fixed
flashlight
flowers
followed
foot
for

forgot
found
four
fours
France
friend
frightened
from
front
full
fun
funny
Gato
gave
get
getting
girl
girls
give
giving
glad
go
going
gold
Gold's
gone
good
got
grass
great
greatest
ground
grow
had
Hal
hands
hanging
happened

happens	hurt	laughed
happy	I	lay
hard	if	lead
harder	in	learn
hardly	Indian	learned
has	Indians	led
have	inside	left
having	into	leg
he	iron	legs
head	is	let
heard	it	liberty
held	its	lift
help	January	lifted
helped	Jim	lifting
helper	Jim's	like
helpers	jump	liked
her	jumped	little
here	jumper	lived
herself	jumping	long
high	just	look
higher	keep	looked
him	keeping	looking
himself	Kentucky	lot
his	kept	loud
hit	kick	love
holding	kicked	loved
home	kicking	made
Hoots	kill	make
Hoots's	killed	makes
hoped	kind	man
horse	kinds	Mancha
horses	king	Mancha's
horse's	knew	many
horses'	know	married
horseshoes	lady	matter
house	large	me
how	last	men
hundred	laugh	might

mile	of	Peter
miles	off	place
minutes	often	places
money	oh	played
more	oil	playing
morning	Oklahoma	plays
most	old	pocket
mother	older	ponies
mountain	on	pony
mountains	once	practice
mouth	one	prettiest
move	only	pretty
moved	onto	prince
moves	open	pull
Mr.	opened	pulled
much	opening	pulling
mule	or	pushed
music	other	pushing
must	out	put
my	outside	putting
name	over	quiet
named	own	quietly
need	owned	race
needed	owner	racehorse
never	owns	races
new	packhorse	rain
New York	parade	raincoat
next	parades	rained
nice	Paris	rainy
night	parked	ran
nights	part	ready
night's	pasture	red
no	Pat	remember
noise	patrol	ride
not	Patsy	rider
nothing	patting	riders
now	people	rides
oats	person	riding

right
ring
ringmaster
river
road
roads
rode
rope
ropes
Rosa
roses
row
run
running
said
same
sat
saved
saw
say
saying
school
schools
seats
see
seemed
seen
seesaw
sell
shaking
she
ship
shoes
shoulders
shouted
show
showed
shows

Shriners
sick
side
silver
sister
sit
sleep
sleepy
small
smart
smile
Smythe
so
some
someday
someone
something
sometimes
soon
south
St. Louis
stand
standing
stands
start
started
starts
stay
stayed
stepped
stick
still
stood
stop
stopped
stories
story
street

streets
strong
such
suddenly
suit
Sultan
supper
sure
surely
suspenders
swim
tail
tails
take
talk
talked
talking
taught
teach
teacher
tease
teased
teeth
tell
tells
ten
tent
than
that
the
their
theirs
them
then
there
these
they
thing

things
think
thinking
this
those
thought
three
threw
through
throw
tied
time
times
tired
to
together
told
too
took
trade
traded
train
trained
trainer
tree
trick
tricks
tried
trip
trunk
try
trying
Tschiffely
turn
turned
two
twos

umbrella
understand
United States
until
up
upon
U-See-It
U-See-It's
very
wagon
wagons
walk
walked
walking
want
wanted
was
watch
watched
watching
water
way
ways
Webb
well
went
were
wet
what
when
where
which
whip
whistle
white
who
whoa

whoever
whose
wide
wife
wild
will
win
winner
with
without
woman
won
wondered
wonderful
woods
word
world
wore
work
worked
workhorses
world
would
wrote
year
years
yellow
you
your